SOMETIMES
I'M JEALOUS

A Read-Together Book for Parents & Children

Sometimes I'm Jealous

by Jane Werner Watson

Robert E. Switzer, M.D.
Former Director of the Children's Division
The Menninger Clinic

J. Cotter Hirschberg, M.D.
William C. Menninger Distinguished Professor of Psychiatry
The Menninger Clinic

with pictures by Irene Trivas

Crown Publishers, Inc.   New York

A Read-Together Book for Parents and Children™
Created in cooperation with The Menninger Foundation

The Dorothy Wright Treatment and Endowment Fund defrays a part of the care
and treatment cost at the Children's Division
of The Menninger Clinic, Box 829, Topeka, Kansas 66601.
Part of the income from the sale of this book goes to that fund.

Library of Congress Cataloging-in-Publication Data. Watson, Jane Werner, 1915– Sometimes I'm jealous. (A Read-together book for parents and children) Summary: A small child learns to accept the new baby in the house. 1. Jealousy in children—Juvenile literature. 2. Sibling rivalry—Juvenile literature. [1. Emotions. 2. Brothers and sisters] I. Switzer, Robert E., 1918– . II. Hirschberg, J. Cotter, 1915– . III. Trivas, Irene, ill. IV. Title. V. Series. BF723.J4W37 1986 152.4
85-17408 ISBN 0-517-56062-3
10 9 8 7 6 5 4 3 2 1
First Edition

NOTE TO PARENTS

Ideally each newborn child is a wanted baby and is for some time made the center of his* small world. Until he is about three or four months old, the baby is not really aware of the difference between himself and his world. When he does become conscious of Mommy—or whoever "mothers" him—as a separate person, he feels that she exists just for him. By seven months, he is aware not only of Mommy and Daddy and their special importance to him but of other people as well; he becomes anxious in the presence of unfamiliar people. Warm, familiar comforting usually reassures him that all is well around him and that he can still feel in control.

Inevitably, though, Baby experiences the disappointing realization of not being in complete control of his world. He feels hungry, and food is not always instantly produced. He wakens, and the one who comforts him is not always in view. He wants to be held and no one is at hand to pick him up at once. He wets and has to wait a while for dry clothing.

Gradually Baby learns that even though he may have to wait for what he wants, he can count on Mommy and Daddy. As the toddler's development continues, his world expands, but

---

*The authors use *he*, *him*, and *his* for simplicity instead of the somewhat awkward *he or she*, *his or her*, and *him or her*, but with no suggestion of preference implied.

he continues to see himself as its center, with everything circling around him and belonging to him.

By the time he is walking and using words, though, the child has learned he cannot always have things his way, that other children—and grown-ups—have wishes as strong as his. He has learned that some experiences are painful and make him cry. These are important lessons to learn. If the child comes to them with a basic trust carried over from the early months when he was the center of his secure little world, he will learn the lessons and not be defeated by them. He will retain his sense of security.

The child will come to know that some things he does please Mommy and Daddy. Other things irritate or anger them. He needs to know that even when his parents are angry, they still love him. Soon he learns to value their praise when he does things that please them. He still thinks of himself before thinking of others, though, so he naturally sometimes does things Mommy and Daddy do not like.

The small child resents anything—such as competition with other children—that diminishes his importance. Not surprisingly, then, learning that Mommy is going to have a new baby makes him feel that he is being displaced. He hears talk about the new baby; much is made of getting ready for it. As Mommy is now more than usually concerned about herself and her health, and Daddy is more concerned about Mommy, the child tends to feel left out.

Letting the youngster take part in preparations and share

in the plans will lessen this jealousy, and he may even pretend that Mommy is having the baby just for him to play with. The facts remain, though: Mommy will almost certainly be going away to give birth to the new baby. When they return, the new baby will take time, love, and attention. This will mean a great change in the child's self-centered world.

Daddy can play a strong part in helping the child to accept the change happily by making it clear to the worried youngster that his love is warm and unchanged. When symptoms of jealousy—overt resentment of the baby or regression to infantile patterns—appear, as they may, they should be met with affectionate reassurance. With thoughtful advance preparation by his parents—helped perhaps by rereadings and discussions of this book—the child will come through this crisis of growth happily. He will realize that he is not alone in his feelings—or "bad"—but that others have the same difficulty he has in accepting change. He will also come to realize that learning to share is a part of growing up. He will be secure enough of his own place so that he can help the new baby to enjoy being the center of its small world just as he once was—and no longer needs to be.

ROBERT E. SWITZER, M.D.

Former Director of the Children's Division
The Menninger Clinic

J. COTTER HIRSCHBERG, M.D.

William C. Menninger Distinguished Professor of Psychiatry
The Menninger Clinic

Do you know what I like?
I like having my own way.
I like getting what I want,
right now,
not having to wait my turn.
I like having Mommy and Daddy
pay attention to me—
nobody else, just me!

I guess when I was a baby
I got my way most of the time.
I can't really remember
that far back
but I guess
I was really the center of things.

Someone was always there
to hold me
and give me what I wanted.
When I was hungry, I was fed.
When I was full, I was burped.
When I was wet or had a b.m.,
my diaper was changed.

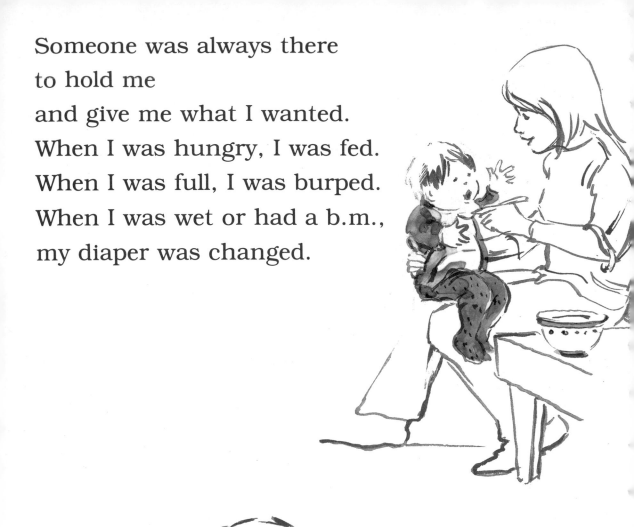

If I felt lonesome, I cried.
Then somebody held me
and I felt better.

If I wanted something,
I grabbed for it.
I didn't think
about anyone but me.

Later I learned that some things
I did made Mommy and Daddy
unhappy with me.
When they were unhappy
they seemed further away,
and I felt upset.

I learned that other things I did
made them happy—
things like learning to eat new foods
and giving up the bottle,
things like waiting to go
to the bathroom.
It was fun to be able to do things
that made them happy.
Then they seemed warm and close,
and I felt happy too.

Sometimes another child came to play.
The other child wanted to be
the center of things too.
He wanted the toys
when he wanted them,
without waiting his turn.
I wanted them too!

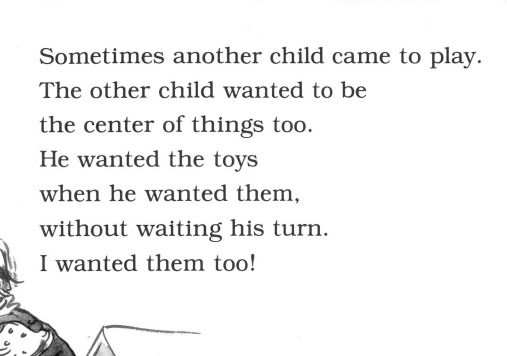

If he fell down and cried,
Mommy held him
to make him feel better.
I felt left out and hurt.
I felt jealous.
But that was just once
in a while.

Then Mommy and Daddy told me
we were going to have
a new baby in our house.

At first I didn't know
what they meant.
I was the new baby
in our house.
I thought it would
always be that way.
Then I thought
they were getting the baby
to be a plaything for me.
I thought Mommy and I
would take care of it together.
Mommy and I would still
be together all the time.
I would still be the center of things.

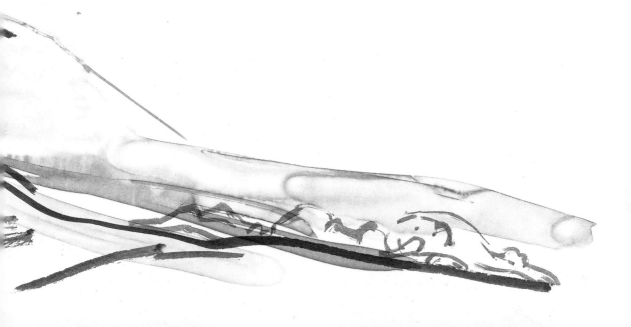

But even before the baby came,
things began to be different.
Mommy didn't feel good sometimes.
She didn't feel like playing
with me then.

She got cross and tired.
Daddy said she was not her usual self.
He did things for her
and sometimes forgot about me.

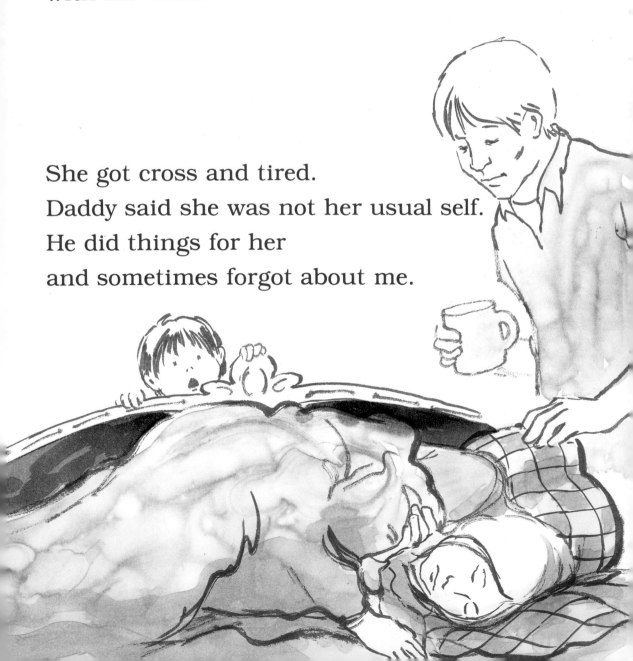

Mommy and Daddy bought lots of things
for the new baby.
Some were toys I wanted to play with.
They didn't let me.
They brought the crib I slept in
when I was a baby
down from the attic.
They fixed up my baby room
for the new baby.

I was glad I was getting big
and wasn't a baby anymore.
Mommy and Daddy were glad too.
But I wasn't all glad.
I wasn't in the center anymore.
I felt jealous.

All this time Mommy's tummy
was getting bigger because the new baby
was growing inside her.
I could tell it was there
because Mommy let me feel her tummy
when the baby moved and kicked.
Daddy was pleased
about the new baby coming.
He had helped Mommy start it.
But I wanted him to be pleased with me.

I wondered how the new baby
would get out of Mommy's tummy.
Mommy said the baby would come out
through a special opening
between her legs.
I was born that way too.
Mommy said she would go
to the hospital to have the new baby.
She said mothers go to the hospital
to have new babies
so the doctors can help
when the baby is ready to be born.

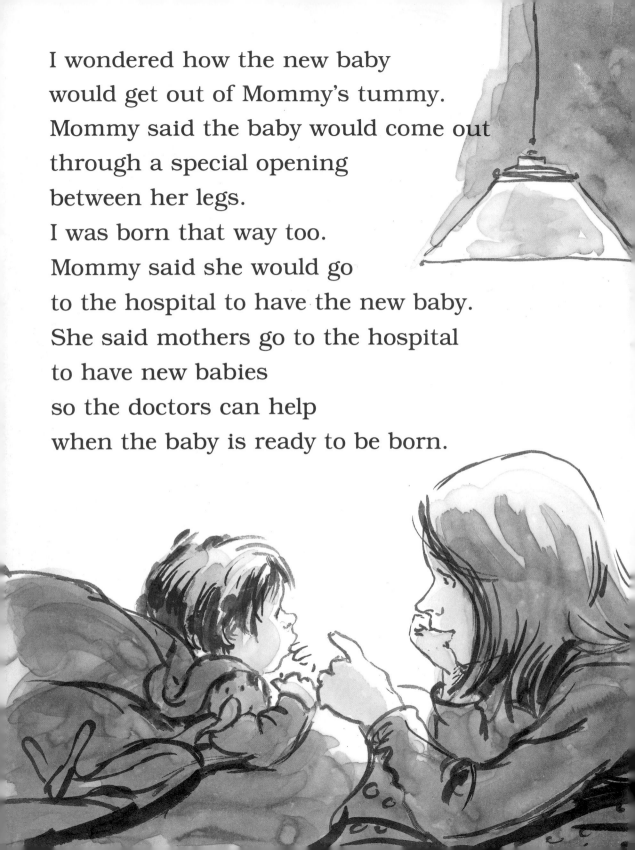

I know about the hospital.
I said I'd visit her there.
Mommy said that would be fine,
and I could meet the new baby.
I could tell she was thinking more
about the new baby than she was about me.
I felt left out.
I felt jealous.

Sometimes I wished there were no new baby.
I wished things could be
like they had been.
I wanted to be the center of things again.
Daddy said someone nice
would stay with me
when he took Mommy to the hospital.
He said it would be someone I knew
like my baby-sitter or my grandma.
But I still didn't like it.
I felt sad and mad.

One day Mommy said,
"Please come and help me
pack a bag for the hospital.
I don't know just when this baby
will be ready to come.
I don't know when
I will have to go."
I helped her pack.
I put in one of my stuffed animals
to keep her company.
She said she would miss me.

Then the time came.
The baby was ready to come.
Mommy and Daddy went to the hospital.
I cried because I felt left out.
I knew where Mommy was, and why,
but I wanted her home with me.

Then the telephone rang.
It was for me.
It was Daddy calling
to tell me the baby was born.
He said Mommy and the baby were fine.
They were taking a nap.

Later Daddy drove me to the hospital.
On the way he said, "Having this new baby
in the family
will be a change for us all.
I know you are not sure
how you feel about it right now.
But we have enough love
to give to the new baby
and still have plenty for you."

When we got to Mommy's room,
she had the new baby in her arms.
I was ready for a big hug,
because I'd missed her,
and I thought she'd missed me.
But she just wanted to show me
the new baby.
Oh, she kissed me
and she told me my stuffed toy
had been a big help to her.
She said the new baby liked it, too.
I wasn't sure how I felt about that.
It was my toy.

Then she showed me the new baby.
It really wasn't much.
Mostly it was a bundle of baby clothes.
It didn't look like anybody.
It couldn't talk or do anything
but eat and sleep and fill its diapers.
But Mommy and Daddy acted as if
it were something wonderful.
I felt left out.

People came to see the new baby.
They brought presents for it.
All they talked about was that baby.
Some of them didn't even see me.
The new baby was the center
of everything, it seemed.
I felt left out.
I wanted to be noticed too,
so I tried acting like the baby.
It didn't really work, though.
I didn't really want to be a baby again.

I like to talk and walk
and play and learn new things.
New babies can't do any of that.
Daddy and Mommy are so pleased
with all the things that I can do.
They say it will be a long time
before the baby can do
all I can do now.
By then, I'll be way ahead of it.
Mommy lets me go outside to play.
The baby can't do that.
I play with other children.
I like that better all the time.
The baby can't do that.
When I come in,
Mommy and Daddy
are glad to see me.

The baby takes a lot of time
and gets in the way sometimes.
But Mommy still loves me.
Daddy still loves me.
And I like the baby too,
now that I know
it hasn't pushed me out
of my place in the family.
I'm still me,
and I'm growing up,
and I like it.